Close Reading 7-9

Comprehension, Interpretation and Language Activities

MARY M FIRTH
and
ANDREW G RALSTON

HODDER GIBSON
PART OF HACHETTE LIVRE UK

The Publishers would like to thank the following for permission to reproduce copyright material:

Photo credits
Page 38 © Paramount Pictures/The Kobal Collection/Wood, Suzy; page 41 © TongRo Image Stock/Alamy; page 47 © isifa Image Service s.r.o./Alamy; page 49 Delfino Dominique/Sunset/Rex Features; page 57 © BL Images Ltd/Alamy; page 59 © Markos Dolopikos/Alamy; page 85 © Dod Miller/Alamy; page 94 © Theo Allofs/Corbis; page 95 © Ron Buskirk/Alamy; page 98 GK Hart/Vikki Hart/Getty Images; page 101 © Oso Media/Alamy; page 115 Stephen Meddle/Rex Features.

Acknowledgements
Extracts from *Tom's Birthday Treat* by John Priest. Reprinted by permission of Pearson Education; extracts from *Only a Show* by Anne Fine. Reprinted by permission of Puffin Books; extracts from *Stranger Danger* by Anne Fine. Reprinted by permission of Puffin Books; extracts from *Charlotte's Web* by E. B. White. Reprinted by permission of Puffin Books; extracts from *Marzipan Max* by Alexander McCall Smith. Reprinted by permission of David Higham Associates; extracts from *Danny Fox Meets a Stranger* by David Thomson. Reprinted by permission of Martina Thomson; extracts from *The Perfect Hamburger* by Alexander McCall Smith. Reprinted by permission of Puffin Books; extracts from *The Story of Walt Disney* by Adele Richardson, Smart Apple Media 2004; extracts from *Cats* by David Alderton. Reprinted by permission of Dorling Kindersley; extracts from *Football and its Followers* by Pete May. Reprinted by permission of Franklin Watts; extracts from *Invaders: The Romans in Scotland* by Richard Dargie. Reprinted by permission of Hodder and Stoughton Limited; extracts from *Modern Scotland: Scotland in the Second World War* by Richard Dargie. Reprinted by permission of Hodder and Stoughton Limited; extracts from *Dinosaurs* by Neil Clark. Reprinted by permission of Dorling Kindersley; extracts from *World of Festivals* by Philip Steele, Hodder and Stoughton Limited 2001; extracts from *Look and Wonder: Dragons* by Gerald Legg. Reprinted by permission of Hodder and Stoughton Limited.

Every effort has been made to trace all copyright holders, but if any have been inadvertently overlooked the Publishers will be pleased to make the necessary arrangements at the first opportunity.

Orders: please contact Bookpoint Ltd, 130 Milton Park, Abingdon, Oxon OX14 4SB. Telephone: (44) 01235 827720. Fax: (44) 01235 400454. Lines are open 9.00 – 5.00, Monday to Saturday, with a 24-hour message answering service. Visit our website at www.hoddereducation.co.uk. Hodder Gibson can be contacted direct on: Tel: 0141 848 1609; Fax: 0141 889 6315; email: hoddergibson@hodder.co.uk

First published in 2008 by
Hodder Gibson, an imprint of Hodder Education,
An Hachette Livre UK Company,
2a Christie Street
Paisley PA1 1NB

Impression number	5	4	3	2	1
Year	2012	2011	2010	2009	2008

Cover illustrations by Mandy Sinclair

Illustrations by Mandy Sinclair and the Richard Duszczak Cartoon Studio Limited

Typeset in Geometric 415 Lt Bt 14.5 pt by Fakenham Photosetting Limited

Printed in Italy

A catalogue record for this title is available from the British Library

ISBN-13: 978 0340 96652 5

Contents

Part Two: Reading (Information)

Introduction to the Teacher

This book is designed to provide an introduction to Close Reading (comprehension) for pupils in lower primary years.

Passages vary in difficulty from Level B to Level C, with the easier passages at the beginning of each section. Half of the passages are narrative (fiction) and half are informative (non-fiction).

The follow up 'Taking a closer look' sections focus on some aspect of language or literature which is highlighted in the passage. This enables the child to be introduced to these features of writing in a natural and unforced manner. They include very simple explanations of elements of basic grammar such as parts of speech or punctuation. However more apparently sophisticated aspects of writing such as setting and characterisation are also introduced here in a way which is accessible to younger pupils. The English Language 5-14: Curriculum and Assessment in Scotland National Guidelines document has been kept in mind while compiling this book.

Since classroom resources do not always permit answer sheets to be used on a once-only basis, this book contains questions in a format which will allow pupils to answer on paper or in their own workbooks. This will enable the books to be recycled for future year groups.

In cloze or space-filling exercises, teachers can use their own discretion in deciding whether pupils should write out sentences or paragraphs in full or simply write down the answers. Such decisions could depend on the time available to complete the work or the speed at which particular pupils can write.

The teacher's book which accompanies this volume contains photocopiable answer sheets on which pupils can write their answers directly, using techniques such as underlining, ticking boxes, or filling in gaps. The format is similar to that used in the National Tests and will enable pupils to complete the tests more quickly. The teacher's book also contains marking schemes.

MMF/ AGR

Getting Started

Why do we have to answer questions and do tests?
The questions make you think about the story and the words and sentences in it.
If you think about what they mean, you will understand the story better and then you will enjoy it even more.
What if I don't know a word? I won't be able to answer the question!
Don't miss out any questions! What do you think you could do?
You could look up the word in a dictionary.
You could ask the teacher.
Or you could ask your Mum and Dad if you were at home.
You could do all of these.
But the best way is to try to work out the meaning for yourself!
Often you can work out quite long and difficult words.
Don't give up!
Try these exercises for practice. You can discuss them with a partner, and we'll see who gets the best answer.

For practice

Think about how you can work out the meaning of the underlined words.

1 Peter Smith was a giant. He was so tall he could not get through the door without bending his head. He was about a foot taller than anyone else in the room.

'Giant' must mean 'a very big person' because

____

2 The pasta was delicious. Everyone had a second helping and said it was the best they had ever tasted. The dish was scraped clean at the end of the meal!

'Delicious' must mean 'nice to eat' because

____

3 There was a terrible din in the classroom. The children were all talking at once and the teacher was shouting. The bell was ringing loudly at the same time.

A 'din' must be a 'loud and horrible noise' because

____

The passages in the second half of this book give you information.

It is important to read carefully so that you get the facts right!

Answering the questions will help you to do this.

You will have to do some thinking if you are to answer the questions correctly.

Learning to think for yourself is the most important lesson of all.

Think about it!

Part One

Reading (Narrative)

Chapter 1

Tom's Birthday Treat

Reading extract

Tom's dad was taking Tom and two of his friends to the zoo for a birthday treat.

'When you get back it will be time for your party,' said Mum.

'Yippee!' said Tom.

After breakfast, Tom and his dad got into the car. They picked up Sally and Robbie and set off for the zoo.

On the way to the zoo, Tom's dad stopped outside a large shop.

'Why have we stopped here?' asked Tom.

'Don't worry, this won't take long,' said Dad. 'I thought you'd like to have a look round a fancy dress shop. You can all choose a costume to wear at the party this afternoon.'

Inside the shop, Tom, Sally and Robbie looked at all the costumes.

→

Reading extract continued

'Wow!' they said.

Sally tried on a clown's costume. She put on a large orange wig and a big red nose. Everyone laughed.

'Look at me!' said Robbie. 'I'm a robot!' Robbie was wearing a shiny silver costume. It had little coloured buttons and switches on it. He pressed the buttons and flicked the switches. The red, yellow and blue lights on his helmet started flashing. He looked just like a robot.

Tom had chosen an astronaut's costume. It had a helmet with a visor.

Tom wanted to show his dad their costumes. They looked round the shop but they couldn't see him.

Suddenly, Tom's dad jumped out from behind a curtain.

'ROOARR!' he growled.

'Don't worry, Sally,' said Tom. 'It's only my dad in a lion's costume playing a trick on us.'

(From *'Tom's Birthday Treat'* by John Priest)

Questions

Section A

Write down each sentence and choose the best ending from the box. The first one is done for you, shown by a star *.

1 Tom was taken to the zoo by

his mum.
his dad.*
his aunt.

2 Tom was having his birthday party

after breakfast.
after school.
after going to the zoo.

3 On the way to the zoo, Tom's dad picked up of Tom's friends.

- one
- two
- three

4 The colour of Sally's wig was

- orange.
- red.
- black.

5 The colour of Robbie's costume was

- blue.
- silver.
- yellow.

6 Tom could not find his dad because

- he had left the shop.
- he was at the zoo.
- he was behind the curtain.

7 When Tom's dad came back again, he

- growled.
- laughed.
- screamed.

Section B

Which costume did each person choose at the fancy dress shop?

Choose a word from the passage.

1 Sally dressed as a ________________.

2 Robbie dressed as a ________________.

3 Tom dressed as a ________________.

4 Tom's dad dressed as a ________________.

Section C

Choose **one word** from the box to fill each space below.

Your teacher will tell you if you need to write out the whole paragraph or just the missing words.

train	zoo	party	dress	quiet	treat	costume
loud	shop	trick	car			

Tom's dad was taking Tom and his friends to the ____1____ for a birthday ____2____.

They travelled there by ____3____.

On the way they stopped at a large ____4____ to choose a ____5____ to wear at the birthday ____6____ .

Tom's dad dressed up as well as the children and played a ____7____ on them. He jumped out at them and made a ____8____ roar.

Section D

These sentences are in the wrong order.

Write down the letters to show the order the sentences come in the story. The first letter that you need is **C**, shown by a star*.

A Then they set off for the zoo.

B Everyone laughed when Sally dressed up.

C Tom had his breakfast with his dad. *

D On the way they stopped to choose a fancy dress outfit.

Taking a closer look

The right order

Often you are asked to put things in the right order.

For practice

Read this story about what Anna does when she gets home from school.

As soon as I get home from school I have a snack to eat. Next, I change out of my school clothes and then I take my dog for a walk. We usually go to the park nearby. After that, I come home again and watch TV until tea time.

Now, think about these questions:

1 What is the first thing Anna does when she gets home?

2 After changing her clothes, what does Anna do next?

3 What is the last thing Anna does before she has her tea?

Write down **three** sentences which answer these questions.

Put Anna's actions in the right order!

Chapter 2

Only a Show

Reading extract

Miss Henry said, 'On Monday, I want every single person in the class to give a little show.'

'Everyone?'

'Give a little show?'

'What sort of show?'

'Any sort of show,' said Miss Henry. 'I'm sure everyone in this room can do something. You could sing a song, or do a dance, or show us some acrobatics or you could give a little five-minute speech about your pet, or what you did in the holidays.'

She picked up the chalk.

'I'm going to write everyone's name on the blackboard,' she said. 'When you have given us your little show, I'll rub it out.'

→

Reading extract continued

Anna watched as Miss Henry's stick of chalk squeaked its way across the blackboard, writing up names: Philip, Asha, Laura, James, Stephen, Talitha, Anna!

There it was, then. In black and white. No chance of getting out of giving a show unless she crept back into the classroom after school, and rubbed it off herself.

But that would leave a gap in all the names, because Miss Henry was just carrying on: William, Moira, Rohan, Suzie, Arif . . .

So many of them! What would everyone do? They weren't circus children. They weren't at an acting school. They were just perfectly normal. What sort of show could they give? What would they do?

(From '*Only a Show*' by Anne Fine)

Questions

Section A

Write down each sentence and choose the best ending from the box.

1 Miss Henry wanted everyone in the class to

> sing a song.
> do a dance.
> put on some kind of show.

2 One thing Miss Henry suggested they could do was

> bring in their pet.
> give a short talk.
> write on the blackboard.

3 After the pupils had given their little show, Miss Henry would

> call out their names.
> write their names on the board.
> rub their names out.

4 Anna wanted to rub her name off the board because

> the names were in the wrong order.
> she didn't want to give a show.
> her name was in black and white.

5 The children who went to the school were

from a circus.
learning to be actors.
ordinary children.

6 Anna was worried because

she couldn't think of anything to do.
she thought the class would laugh at her.
she didn't like Miss Henry.

Section B

Write down the answers to these questions. You may use your own words or words from the passage.

1 Miss Henry said the class would do their show on ________.

2 She suggested they could talk about what they did ________.

3 A word that describes the noise the chalk made on the board is ________.

4 What did Anna think of doing to get out of putting on a show?

5 Why would this idea not work?

Section C

These sentences are in the wrong order.

Write down the letters to show the order the sentences come in the story.

The first letter that you need is **C**, shown by a star *.

A She could go back after school and rub out her name.

B She wrote everyone's name on the board.

C Miss Henry asked everyone in the class to put on a show. *

D She said she would rub out the names after each pupil had given his or her show.

E Anna could only think of one way of getting out of giving her show.

Taking a closer look

Capital Letters and Full Stops

A sentence has a capital letter at the start and a full stop at the end.

A capital letter is also used for names of people, towns, and so on.

For practice

Write out each of these sentences and put in full stops and capital letters.

1 the name of anna's teacher was miss henry

2 anna was not looking forward to doing her talk

3 stephen, philip and james were three boys in anna's class

4 there was a girl in the class called laura

5 the book about anna was written by anne fine

6 i like the harry potter books

7 aberdeen and glasgow are two large cities in scotland

8 the flight to america leaves from prestwick

9 hampden park is scotland's national football stadium

10 edinburgh is the capital of scotland

Chapter 3

Stranger Danger

Reading extract

On Monday morning a policeman came to Joe's class to show everybody a film and give them a talk.

The film was called *Stranger Danger*. Joe didn't see much of it. He was under the table, trying to coax a baby daddy-long-legs on to the palm of his hand. He heard a bit of the film, though. He heard, *Never take sweets from a stranger*, and, *Never go with a stranger*. Joe thought the baby daddy-long-legs must have seen the same film. It wouldn't put even one step on Joe's hand, and Joe didn't like to pick it up in case one of its legs fell off.

Afterwards, the policeman spoke to everybody. He was good fun, and made a lot of jokes. Mostly he talked about being careful.

"Don't worry about being too careful," he said. "You can't be too careful. You have to use your common sense. Now, let's hear from everybody. What is the first safety rule?"

→

Reading extract continued

"Never take sweets from a stranger!" everyone chanted.

"Right!" said the policeman. "And that means food and drink and anything at all that goes in your mouth."

He paused, and stuck his thumb in his mouth like a baby. Everyone giggled.

He took his thumb out and looked serious again.

"And what is the other safety rule?" he asked.

"Never go with a stranger," everyone chanted.

Reading extract continued

"I can't hear you," he said, cupping his ears and looking puzzled.

"*Never go with a stranger!*" everyone shouted.

"I still can't hear," he said. "You'll have to speak up. I must be going a bit deaf."

"NEVER GO WITH A STRANGER," everyone bellowed.

"That's good," he said. "Now don't forget!"

And winking goodbye at Joe's teacher, Mrs Murray, he settled his helmet back on his head, and went off.

Joe looked down at the floor again, but, frightened by the noise, his baby daddy-long-legs had disappeared.

(From *'Stranger Danger?'* by Anne Fine)

Questions

Section A

Write down each sentence and choose the best ending from the box.

1 Joe did not pick up the daddy-long-legs because

- he did not want to touch it.
- he could not catch it.
- one of its legs might fall off.

C

2 During most of his visit to Joe's class, the policeman

- told jokes.
- chatted to the pupils.
- talked about being careful.

C

3 Joe did not see much of the film because

- he was not interested in it.
- he was under the table.
- he was holding the daddy-long-legs in his hand.

B

4 After showing the film, the policeman spoke

- to Joe.
- to everybody.
- to Mrs Murray, the teacher.

B

5 The daddy-long-legs disappeared because

- Joe was looking down at it.
- it was frightened by the noise.
- Joe had tried to pick it up.

6 When the class chanted the policeman's safety rule, he

- pretended he couldn't hear them.
- covered his ears.
- asked them to repeat it.

Section B

Which of the following sentences are true and which are false?

Write **true** or **false** for each one.

1 Joe watched all of the film. ________

2 Joe heard some parts of the film. ________

3 Joe was more interested in playing with the daddy-long-legs. ________

4 The policeman was serious all the time. ________

5 Sometimes the policeman was funny. ________

6 Sometimes the policeman was serious. ________

Section C

Write down the answers to these questions. You may use your own words or words from the passage.

1 The policeman came to Joe's class to do **two** things. What were they?

2 What was the **first** safety rule the policeman had to give the children?

3 What was the policeman's **second** safety rule?

4 Why did Joe think the daddy-long-legs must have seen the safety film shown by the policeman?

5 Write down some words which show that the class **liked** the policeman.

6 Write down **one** thing the policeman did that made the class laugh.

Section D

Write down **a single word** from the passage which fits each of the following meanings.

1 to persuade

2 repeated something together

3 not able to hear

4 shouted loudly

Section E

These sentences are in the wrong order.

Write down the letters to show the order the sentences come in the story.

The first letter that you need is **D**, shown by a star *.

A On the way out, the policeman winked at Miss Murray.

B He showed the class a film and talked to them about safety rules.

C After the talk, the policeman put his helmet back on.

D A policeman came to Joe's class on Monday morning. *

Taking a closer look

Question Marks

A Question mark looks like this: ?

Some of the sentences in '*Stranger Danger*' end with a question mark.

When you are asking a question, put a question mark at the end of the sentence.

For example,

For practice

Write out each sentence, putting a question mark at the end of the ones which are questions.

If the sentence is not a question, put a full stop.

1 what was the film called

2 i can't remember

3 did you listen to what the policeman said

4 i listened to part of his talk

5 it will soon be my birthday

6 when will it be your birthday

7 did you know you had won the prize

8 my teacher has just told me

9 how are you today

10 i'm feeling great, thanks

Chapter 4

Charlotte's Web

Reading extract

Wilbur the pig was lonely after being moved to a farm where he did not know anyone. One night in the barn he heard a little voice offering to be his friend.

At last Wilbur saw the creature that had spoken to him in such a kindly way. Stretched across the top of the doorway was a big spider's web, and hanging from it, head down, was a large grey spider. She had eight legs, and she was waving one of them at Wilbur. "See me now?" she asked.

"Oh, yes indeed," said Wilbur. "Yes indeed! How are you? Good morning! Very pleased to meet you. What is your name, please?"

"My name," said the spider, "is Charlotte."

"I think you're beautiful," said Wilbur.

"Yes, I am pretty," replied Charlotte. "Now, watch me wrap up this fly."

→

Reading extract continued

A fly that had been crawling along Wilbur's trough had flown up and blundered into the lower part of Charlotte's web and was tangled in the sticky threads. The fly was beating its wings furiously trying to break loose and free itself. "First," said Charlotte, "I dive at him." She plunged headfirst towards the fly. As she dropped, a tiny silk thread unwound from her rear end.

"Next, I wrap him up." She grabbed the fly, threw a few jets of silk round it, and rolled it over and over, wrapping it so that it couldn't move. Wilbur watched in horror. He could hardly believe what he was seeing, and although he detested flies he was sorry for this one.

Reading extract continued

"There!" said Charlotte. "Now I knock him out so he'll be more comfortable." She bit the fly. "He can't feel a thing now," she remarked. "He'll make a perfect breakfast for me."

"You mean you eat flies?" gasped Wilbur.

"Certainly. Flies, bugs, grasshoppers, beetles, moths, butterflies, daddy-long-legs – anything that is careless enough to get caught in my web. I have to live, don't I?"

"Why, yes, of course," said Wilbur. "Do they taste good?"

"Delicious. I'm not entirely happy about my diet of flies and bugs, but it's the way I'm made."

Wilbur was sad because his new friend was so bloodthirsty.

"I can't help it," said Charlotte. "All of us spiders do it."

"It's cruel," replied Wilbur.

(From *'Charlotte's Web'* by E. B. White)

Questions

Section A

Write down each sentence and choose the best ending from the box.

A Wilbur was looking for the creature because

> it had waved to him.
> it was hanging head down.
> it had spoken to him in a kindly way.

B The first thing Wilbur wanted to know was

> how the spider caught flies.
> what the spider's name was.
> what the spider liked to eat.

C The fly had got tangled in the web because

the threads of the web were sticky.
Charlotte had grabbed it.
it was crawling on Wilbur's trough.

D Charlotte wrapped the fly in silk in order to

knock it out.
keep the fly from moving.
roll it round and round.

E Charlotte caught flies because

all spiders do this.
she enjoyed chasing flies.
flies were easy to find.

Section B

These sentences are in the wrong order.

Write down the letters to show the order the sentences come in the story.

The first letter that you need is **C**, shown by a star *.

A Charlotte bit the fly to knock it out.

B Charlotte wrapped up the fly in silk threads.

C A fly was crawling on Wilbur's trough. *

D Charlotte dived down and grabbed the fly.

E The fly flew up and got stuck in Charlotte's web.

Section C

Decide whether Charlotte or Wilbur or **neither** of them would be likely to say these words.

	Charlotte	Wilbur	Neither Charlotte or Wilbur
1 "Perhaps the creature who spoke so kindly will be my friend."			
2 "I am very good at catching flies."			
3 "I like eating flies but I don't like grasshoppers or beetles."			
4 "I shall try eating flies, too, if they taste so good."			
5 "I think catching flies is cruel."			

Section D

1 Which **phrase** tells you Wilbur had been looking for the kind creature for a long time?

2 Pick out and write down **two** words which describe the **colour** and **size** of the spider.

3 Pick out **a phrase** (a group of words) which tells you that the fly tried hard to escape from the web.

4 The word **'detested'** tells you that Wilbur usually

felt sorry for flies.
hated flies.
ate flies.

Write down the best answer from the box.

5 The word **'gasped'** tells you that Wilbur felt that Charlotte ate flies.

angry
shocked
happy

Write down the best answer from the box.

Section E

Write down the words which are needed to complete the story. You may use words from the story or your own words.

A large grey spider was _____1_____ from a spider's web stretched across the _____2_____ . She _____3_____ to Wilbur with one of her _____4_____ legs. She said her _____5_____ was Charlotte. A fly had got _____6_____ in the sticky threads of her web. Charlotte wrapped up the fly in _____7_____. When it could not move she _____8_____ the fly so that it could not feel a thing. Charlotte wanted to have the fly for _____9_____. Although he liked having Charlotte for his friend, Wilbur thought that catching flies was _____10_____.

Taking a closer look

Speech Marks

Speech marks look like this: **“ ”**

In the story, Charlotte the spider talks to Wilbur the pig. How can you tell they are talking?

- The words each creature says are put inside speech marks like this:

  "Oh, yes indeed," said Wilbur.

Speech marks are also called **inverted commas**. 'Inverted' means upside down.

Look carefully at the speech marks before and after words.

Do you think 'inverted commas' is a good name for them?

★ When someone stops speaking and another person speaks, the words go in a new line, even if there is space left over:

"I think you're beautiful," said Wilbur.

"Yes, I am pretty," said Charlotte.

One more thing to remember!

You need to put a punctuation mark **after** the words spoken, but **before** the speech marks. It is usually a comma, but it could be something else, like a question mark.

For practice (1)

Write out these sentences, and put speech marks **round the words spoken**.

1. I hate spiders, said Susan.
2. My dog is a Collie, explained Mark.
3. My Dad loves his car, laughed Miranda.
4. How old are you? asked Joe.
5. I'm nine, answered Anna.

Did you remember that the punctuation mark goes **inside** the speech marks?

For practice (2)

Simon and Paul were arguing about football. Write out their conversation, putting in the speech marks. Start **a new line** every time a different boy speaks.

> *Which team do you support? asked Paul. Rangers are my best team, answered Simon. I like Celtic better, said Paul. Rangers won the cup last year, boasted Simon. But Celtic deserved to win, argued Paul.*

Have you noticed. . .?

Speech marks can be double ". . ."
or
single '. . .'

Chapter 5

Ralph S. Mouse

Reading extract

Part 1

The night wind, moaning and whistling, dashed snow against the windows of the Mountain View Inn. Inside, a fire crackled in the stone fireplace. The grandfather clock, as old and tired as the inn itself, marked time with a slow *tick. . .tock. . .* that seemed to say, "Wait. . .ing, wait. . .ing."

Reading extract continued

Everyone in the lobby was waiting – the desk clerk; old Matt, the handyman, who also carried guests' luggage to their rooms; Ryan Bramble, the son of the hotel's new housekeeper; and Ralph, the mouse who lived under the grandfather clock.

The desk clerk dozed, waiting for guests who did not arrive. Matt leaned against the wall to watch television while he waited for the desk clerk to close up for the night. Ryan, sitting on the floor to watch television, waited for his mother to tell him to go to bed because he had to go to school the next day. Ralph, crouched beside Ryan, waited for the adults to leave so he could bring out his mouse-sized motor-cycle.

Part 2

On the television set, a sports car crashed into a truck, shot off a cliff, and burst into flames. "Wow!" said Ryan.

"If I had a sports car like that," said Ralph, "I wouldn't let it run off a cliff."

Ralph was an unusual mouse. He had listened to so many children and watched so much television that he had learned to talk. Not everyone could understand

Reading extract continued

him. Those who could were lonely children who shared Ralph's interest in fast cars and motorcycles. Matt was the only adult who understood Ralph.

Mrs Bramble entered the lobby. "Come on, my boy," she said to Ryan. "It's past your bedtime. You know the manager doesn't like you hanging around the lobby."

"Aw, Mom, just let me watch the end of the programme," pleaded Ryan. "I'll leave if any guests arrive."

At that moment, the rattle and crunch of a car with chains on its tyres was heard. Ryan rose and walked backwards out of the lobby so he wouldn't miss the high-speed chase on the television screen. As he left, he gave Ralph a little wave with his fingertips, a wave no one else would notice. Ralph wished Ryan could stay up all night like a mouse.

(From '*Ralph S. Mouse*' by Beverly Cleary)

Questions

Section A

Write down each sentence and choose the best ending from the box.

1 The weather at the inn was

- cold but dry.
- windy and rainy.
- cold and rainy.
- windy and snowy.

2 At the start of the story, in the lobby there were

- three people and one mouse.
- two people and two mice.
- two people and one mouse.
- four people and one mouse.

3 The people in the lobby were

- carrying luggage or watching television.
- dozing or watching television.
- sitting and dozing.
- watching television or speaking to the guests.

4 The programme on the television involved

- mice on motorcycles.
- cars skidding on snow.
- a sports car crashing.
- a truck driver shooting someone.

5 Mrs Bramble told Ryan to go to bed because

- the programme had finished.
- the manager didn't like him being there.
- he was looking very tired.
- he was getting in the way of the guests.

Section B

The answers to these questions can be found in Part 1 of the story.

1 What word gives us the idea that the wind was sounding **like a sad person**?

2 What word gives us the idea of the **sound** the fire was making?

3 In what **two** ways did the grandfather clock seem like the inn?

4 Where did Ralph the mouse live?

5 Which **two** people were watching television?

6 What did Ralph the mouse want to bring out after the adults left?

Section C

The answers to these questions can be found in Part 2 of the story.

1 What **two** things had Ralph done which had helped him learn to speak?

2 Name **two** things which Ralph was interested in.

3 Who was the only **adult** who could understand Ralph?

4 Find a word which means the same as 'begged'.

5 Find **two** words which describe the noise made by the car with chains on its tyres.

Section D

Write down the words which are needed to complete the story. You may use words from the story or your own words.

At the Mountain View Inn the wind ____1____ snow against the windows. Everyone in the lobby was ____2____ for something. Ryan was watching ____3____ while Ralph the mouse ____4____ beside him. The programme showed a ____5____ bursting into flames. Then Mrs Bramble, Ryan's ____6____, came in and told him to go to bed. Ryan begged to stay up and see the end of the programme, but he promised to leave if any ____7____ arrived. Just then, they heard the sound of a car with ____8____ on its tyres. Ryan walked ____9____ out of the lobby so that he could still see the television. As he left he ____10____ to Ralph with his fingertips.

Taking a closer look

Setting

The setting of a story is the place where it happens. If the writer describes the place well, you can imagine it clearly and this helps you to enjoy the story.

The story *'Ralph S. Mouse'* is set in a hotel called the 'Mountain View Inn'. Where do you think a hotel with this name would be?

For practice (1)

Look back at Part 1 of the story again, and then answer the questions.

1. How do you know it is cold outside, but warm and cosy inside?
2. Write down the names of **three** things mentioned which were to be seen inside the inn.
3. Draw a picture of either the **inside** or the **outside** of the Mountain View Inn.

American English

Although many people in the world speak English, their language can be a little different from ours in Britain.

'*Ralph S. Mouse*' is an American story, and it is set in America.

The writer uses some American words and phrases.

For example, he calls the hallway of the hotel the **LOBBY**.

- ★ In Britain, we call the person at the hotel reception desk the **RECEPTIONIST**.
- ★ What name is given to this person in the story?

Hint

You need to find two words.

For practice (2)

Look at Part 2 of the story.

1. Find the American word for lorry.
2. Find the American word for Mum.

For practice (3)

Below is a list of American words and in the box are the words we use for the same things in Britain. Can you match them up? If you are stuck, look up the American word in a dictionary.

1 freeway

2 sneakers

3 soda

4 sidewalk

5 candy

6 railroad

7 pants

8 yard

9 gas

10 bathrobe

sweets	railway	motorway	lemonade
dressing-gown	trousers	garden	petrol
pavement	trainers		

Chapter 6

Marzipan Max

Reading extract

Max lived with his father and mother at the very edge of the village. His father was a farmer and their house, like all the other houses in that area, was really half-barn and half-house. In the cold winters, when the mountain-sides and the valley floor were covered with a thick layer of snow, the cows and the sheep took shelter in the barn side of the house. As he lay in bed at night, Max could hear the sound of the animals in their stalls. It was a comforting sound that always made him feel drowsy and safe.

Just about everyone in the village was a farmer too. Everyone, that is, except for the postman, the grocer and Herr Gross. Herr Gross was a baker, and the village people were very proud of him. Not every village had its own baker, and people would come from all the neighbouring villages up and down the valley to buy the bread baked by Herr Gross.

Max loved to watch Herr Gross mixing the dough for the bread. Sometimes he would help dust each loaf with

Reading extract continued

flour before the large trays were slid into the wood-fired oven. Then, when the bread was done, they would tip it on to racks and leave it to cool until the customers came for it.

'You should become a baker,' Herr Gross said to him. 'You could make a good living.'

'Would you teach me?' Max asked.

Herr Gross laughed. 'I'm too old,' he replied. 'It's as much as I can do to keep up with the demand for my bread. And I can't go on for ever!'

Reading extract continued

Max loved the taste of Herr Gross's bread, and he wondered if the old man was able to make anything else.

'I'll tell you what I was really good at – marzipan. I used to make it when I was learning my trade. My boss was a marvellous marzipan maker – the best in the country, I think. And he taught me some of his tricks. I've never forgotten them, although that was an awful long time ago.'

Max caught his breath.

'Marzipan?' There was nothing he loved to eat more than marzipan. Rich, yellow marzipan, smelling of almonds and tasting even more delicious than chocolate itself. The very thought of it made Max's mouth water.

Herr Gross looked at Max. There was a smile on his face as he dusted his hands on his apron.

'Would you like some?' he asked suddenly.

'There's nothing I'd like more,' Max answered quickly. 'Nothing!'

(From '*Marzipan Max*' by Alexander McCall Smith)

Questions

Section A

Write down each sentence and choose the best ending from the box.

1 The farmhouse where Max lived was

> at the edge of the village.
> on the mountain side.
> in the valley.

2 When Max heard the sound of the animals at night he felt

> very happy.
> sleepy and safe.
> frightened.

3 Almost everyone who lived in the village worked as

> a farmer.
> a postman.
> a baker.

4 People bought bread from Herr Gross because

> not every village had its own baker.
> he made better bread than other bakers.
> people did not like to make their own bread.

5 Herr Gross suggested that Max should become a baker because

Max was good at baking bread.
Max could make a good living.
Herr Gross was too old to keep working as a baker.

6 Max's favourite thing to eat was

bread.
chocolate.
marzipan.

7 When Max thought about his favourite food

it put a smile on his face.
it made his mouth water.
he caught his breath.

Section B

Use words from the passage or your own words to answer these questions.

1 Where did the cows and sheep shelter in the cold winter?

2 Write down one reason why Herr Gross did not want to teach Max to be a baker.

3 Write down two things we are told about marzipan.

Section C

These sentences are in the wrong order.

Write down the letters to show the order the sentences come in the story.

The first letter that you need is **B**, shown by a star *.

A Max asked Herr Gross if he could make anything else apart from bread.

B Max liked to watch Herr Gross baking bread. *

C Max asked Herr Gross if he would teach him to bake.

D Herr Gross told Max he should become a baker.

E Herr Gross said he was very good at making marzipan.

F Herr Gross said he was too old to teach Max and keep up with the demand for bread.

Section D

Find a word from the passage to fill in each of the spaces.

Your teacher will tell you if you need to write out the whole paragraph or just the missing words.

The people who lived in the ______1______ were ______2______ of their baker, Herr Gross. Customers would come from ______3______ villages in other parts of the ______4______ to buy his bread. Max used to watch the baker mixing the ______5______ for the bread.

The bread made by Herr Gross was so popular that he could hardly keep up with the ______6______ .

Taking a closer look

Nouns

'naming words'

Max   flour   tray   loaf   mother   Anna   apron

All the words we use when we talk or write help us understand.

Different kinds of words help in different ways.

The words which tell us the names of things are called NOUNS.

In the story, the name of the boy is 'Max'. The word 'Max' is a noun. Max lived with his father and mother. The words 'father' and 'mother' are nouns, too.

For practice (1)

Read the first paragraph of the story '*Marzipan Max*' again.

Find a word for each of these meanings:

1 A very small town

2 A man who grows crops

3 A building you live in

4 Frozen white flakes which fall from the sky

5 An animal covered in wool

6 Something you sleep in

7 Another word for noise

* The words you have found will all be nouns.

For practice (2)

Can you tell which of these words from the story are also nouns? You must ask, 'Is it the name of something?'

Write down the word. Then write 'yes' if you think the word is a noun, or 'no' if you don't think it is a noun.

	Yes	No
1 postman	☐	☐
2 and	☐	☐
3 was	☐	☐
4 baker	☐	☐
5 bread	☐	☐
6 large	☐	☐
7 laughed	☐	☐

	Yes	No
8 man	☐	☐
9 marzipan	☐	☐
10 eat	☐	☐

For practice

In a group or with a partner, read the last part of the story from 'I'll tell you'.

- ★ Make a list of all the words in this part which you think are nouns.
- ★ Swap your list with another group's list.
- ★ Put a tick at the words you think are nouns and a cross at the words you think are something else.

Now, look over your lists with your teacher to find out who got most nouns right.

Chapter 7

Danny Fox Meets a Stranger

Reading extract

Part 1 Danny's Thoughts

Danny Fox sat on the beach looking up at the mountain where he lived. He could not see his den because it had a secret entrance. It was near the top of the mountain hidden by a hawthorn bush which grew, hanging down like a prickly curtain, from a gap in a large grey rock. Inside the rock there was a small cave which was warm, dry and cosy. This was the secret den where Danny Fox lived with Mrs Doxie Fox and their three children whose

Reading extract continued

names were Lick, Chew and Swallow. Here they would all lie together in the dark, looking down towards the sea through the gaps in the hawthorn twigs, and they would always feel safe because they could watch what went on outside without being seen.

Danny Fox had come down to the beach because he wanted to think. He was thinking about his den. He was wondering whether he could make it wider. Lick, Chew and Swallow grew bigger every day, and now there was only just enough room for the whole family to lie down together. If one of them turned in his sleep, the others would all have to move.

Part 2: The Strange Animal

Danny yawned when he thought about sleep. As he yawned, he made a yowling sound which was carried by the wind all the way up the mountain to his den. The little foxes heard it and looked out. They yelped a reply, but Danny could not hear them because the wind blew the sound of their voices away from him.

But there was a stranger walking on the mountain who heard the yowling yawn of Danny Fox and the yelping of Lick, Chew and Swallow. He was long and lanky, grey

→

Reading extract continued

and shaggy, and three times as large as Danny Fox. He was strong and fierce and a good runner.

Danny Fox's mouth closed with a snap in the middle of the yawn. He had caught sight of this strange animal which was standing on the mountain-side only a few yards from Danny's den. At first he thought it was a shepherd's dog. But he knew all the dogs in the neighbourhood and he had never seen one as big as this. Then, when it began to move again, he knew by its prowling, slouchy, secret way of walking that it was a wolf.

(From '*Danny Fox Meets a Stranger*' by David Thomson)

Questions

Section A

Write down each sentence and choose the best ending from the box.

1 Danny could not see his den because

> it was behind a prickly curtain.
> the entrance was hidden by a bush.
> he was sitting on the beach.

2 Danny's family felt safe in the den because

> there were gaps in the hawthorn twigs.
> they could look down at the sea.
> they could see out without being seen.

3 Danny was thinking about his den because

> it was getting too small for his family.
> it was too wide for his family.
> it had a secret entrance.

4 Danny could not hear the little foxes calling because

> he was scratching up the sand.
> he was digging with his front paws.
> the wind blew the sound away.

5 Danny knew the strange animal was a wolf because

it walked in a slouchy, prowling way.
it was smaller than a shepherd's dog.
it was standing near his den.

Section B

The answers to these questions are in Part 1: Danny's Thoughts.

1 Which word tells us the hawthorn bush had **thorns**?

2 Which **three** words tell us that the small cave was comfortable for the foxes to live in?

3 Find and write down the names of Danny's **three** cubs.

4 Write down **a phrase** which tells us how light it was inside the foxes' den.

Section C

The answers to these questions are in Part 2: The Strange Animal.

1. Which word describes the noise Danny made when he yawned?
2. Which word describes the noise the **little** foxes made?
3. Write down **a phrase** that compares the **size** of the strange animal to Danny.
4. Write down **a phrase** that tells us the strange animal could move **fast**.
5. Which word tells us Danny closed his mouth very suddenly?

Section D

These sentences are in the wrong order.

Write down the letters to show the order the sentences come in the story.

The first letter that you need is **B**, shown by a star *.

A Danny suddenly noticed a strange animal standing near his den.

B Danny went down to the beach to think. *

C When the animal moved he saw it was a wolf.

D The little foxes yelped a reply to Danny.

E He yawned, making a yowling sound.

Section E

Write down the words which are needed to complete the story. You may use words from the story or your own words.

Danny Fox had gone to the _____1_____ to think. He was thinking about making his den _____2_____ since his cubs were growing fast. His den was near the top of the _____3_____ and he could not see its entrance because it was _____4_____ by a hawthorn bush. Danny yowled and the _____5_____ yelped in reply. He could not hear them because of the _____6_____. However, a strange animal which was passing by did _____7_____ them. Danny saw that the strange animal was a _____8_____.

Taking a closer look

Adjectives – describing words

Adjectives are describing words. They tell you more about nouns. They help you to know more about things – how big things are or what colour, or something special about them.

For example, in the phrase 'a tall mountain', 'tall' is an adjective and it tells you the mountain was very high.

For practice (1)

There are lots of adjectives in the story of Danny Fox.

Can you find an adjective from the story to put in each of these spaces? You will find them all in Part 1.

Write out the phrases, putting one adjective in each space.

1 a ____________ bush

2 a ____________ , ____________ rock

3 a ____________ cave which was ____________ ,
____________ and ____________

4 a ____________ den

For practice (2)

Look at the second paragraph in Part 2 of the story.

Write down **six** adjectives the writer uses to describe the **wolf**.

1 ____________ **2** ____________ **3** ____________

4 ____________ **5** ____________ **6** ____________

For practice (3)

Find the opposites!

In Part 2 of the story, the baby foxes are called 'the ***little*** foxes'.

The opposite of 'little' is '***big***'.

Now, write down six words which are **opposite** in meaning to the six you wrote down in the last exercise.

1 ____________ **2** ____________ **3** ____________

4 ____________ **5** ____________ **6** ____________

Hint

One of your words in the last exercise was a colour. Choose the colour which you think is most different.

Chapter 8

The Perfect Hamburger

Reading extract

Old Mr Borthwick has a hamburger shop but not many customers. He and his young friend Joe are trying to find out the name of a spice which they need to make a perfect hamburger. They go to a large hotel to ask its famous Italian chef to help.

Part 1

The Excelsior Hotel was about fifty miles away. When they reached the hotel, Mr Borthwick parked his car in →

Reading extract continued

the car park and together they walked round to the back of the building, where Mr Borthwick said they would find the kitchen entrance. There they were met by a porter, who asked them what they wanted.

"We have come," Mr Borthwick said, "to see Mr Cassaroli."

The porter directed them along a passage and there, in front of them, was a wide door with a notice that said, "Kitchen. No Entry."

Joe had never seen such a magnificent kitchen. Stretching out in front of them were rows and rows of tables and ovens. Extractor fans whirred busily, and steam rose from a dozen different pans. Here and there, standing in front of chopping boards or mixing bowls, men and women dressed all in white were preparing dishes. It was a remarkable sight.

As they entered, everyone suddenly stopped working and stared at them. Then after a few moments, a short and very fat man clapped his hands angrily and everyone returned to work. The fat man waddled across towards Joe and Mr Borthwick.

Reading extract continued

Part 2

“How dare you enter my kitchen!” he shouted. “You must leave immediately!”

And with that he clapped his hands and began to waddle away.

“Excuse me,” Mr Borthwick called out after him. “But I have come to see Mr Cassaroli.”

The chef turned round. “I am the great Cassaroli,” he said impatiently. “What do you want?”

Mr Borthwick began to explain. ”We have heard,” he began rather nervously, “that there is nobody who knows more about spices than you do.”

As Mr Borthwick spoke these words, there was a change in Cassaroli’s manner. The famous chef now smiled. “Yes,” he said. “That is said.”

Mr Borthwick continued. “And we wondered if you could identify a spice for us. We have it here.” Joe passed Mr Borthwick the tin and the old man gave it to the chef.

Reading extract continued

"Let me see, let me see," Cassaroli said impatiently, grabbing the tin from Mr Borthwick's hands. "This should not be difficult."

The chef opened the lid and poked his small fat nose in to sniff at the spice. He looked for a moment, frowned, and took another sniff. He took a small quantity of the spice out of the tin and examined it. Then saying something to himself in Italian, he put a little on his tongue to taste it. "Mmm," he said, thoughtfully.

Mr Borthwick looked hopeful. "Can you tell us what it is?" he asked.

Cassaroli looked embarrassed. "I cannot," he said crossly.

(From '*The Perfect Hamburger*'
by Alexander McCall Smith)

Questions

Section A

Write down each sentence and choose the best ending from the box. The answers come from Part 1 of the passage.

1 Mr Borthwick and Joe travelled to the hotel

by train.
by car.
by bus.

2 The porter told Joe and Mr Borthwick

to go along a passage.
to go away.
to go back to the car-park.

3 Mr Borthwick and Joe entered the hotel

by the back door.
by a side door.
by the front door.

4 When Mr Borthwick and Joe entered the kitchen, the workers

shouted at them.
clapped their hands.
stared at them.

5 The word 'whirred' described the noise made by

the extractor fans.
the pans.
the ovens.

Section B

Who was most likely to have said these things? Choose one person for each of the rows in the table on the next page. The answers come from both parts of the passage. Write down the number and the name.

	The porter	Mr Borthwick	Mr Cassaroli
1 "I do not allow strangers in my kitchen."			
2 "What do you want in this hotel?"			
3 "We are sorry to disturb you."			
4 "I know a lot about spices."			
5 "Can you tell us the name of this spice?"			

Section C

Match the character to the correct ending. Write down the name of the character and the letter of the correct ending.

1 Mr Borthwick ________ 2 Mr Cassaroli ________ 3 Joe ________	A found the kitchen an amazing sight. B knew the name of the spice. C showed hotel visitors where to go. D was a famous chef. E was the manager of the hotel. F felt nervous asking for help.

Section D

These sentences are in the wrong order.

Write down the letters to show the order the sentences come in the story.

The first letter that you need is **C**, shown by a star *.

A Mr Cassaroli admitted that he did not know the name of the spice.

B Mr Cassaroli ordered Joe and Mr Borthwick to leave his kitchen.

C The porter directed Joe and Mr Borthwick to the kitchen. *

D Mr Cassaroli sniffed at the spice and tasted it.

E Mr Borthwick said they had heard Mr Cassaroli knew more about spices than anyone else.

F Mr Cassaroli began to relax and smiled at them.

Section E

There is a summary of the story on the next page. Write down the words which are needed to complete it. You may use words from the story or your own words.

When they arrived at the Hotel, Mr Borthwick and Joe asked a ____1____ the way to the kitchen. He ____2____ them along a passage. Although a ____3____ on the kitchen door said 'No Entry', Joe and Mr Borthwick went in. The chef, Mr Cassaroli, was angry and ____4____ them to leave at once. Mr Borthwick politely ____5____ what they wanted. He said they had heard Mr Cassaroli knew more about ____6____ than anyone else. When he heard this, Mr Cassaroli's ____7____ changed and he smiled. Mr Borthwick asked Mr Cassaroli if he knew the name of the spice they had in the ____8____. Mr Cassaroli thought this would be ____9____ for him to do. However, he was ____10____ because he did not know what the spice was.

Taking a closer look

Characters

The people in a story are known as the **characters**.

In the story *'The Perfect Hamburger'*, there are three main characters: Joe, Mr Borthwick and Mr Cassaroli.

In the story we learn some facts about the characters, such as how old they are, and what they look like, or what their jobs are.

For practice (1)

With a ruler, draw three boxes like the ones below and on the next page. In each box, write down all the facts you can find about the character.

Hint

The introduction to the story will help you.

You could do this with a partner.

Joe

Mr Borthwick

Mr Cassaroli

As well as learning **facts** about a character, you can also find out what **kind of person** the character is. Then you can decide if you **like** the character or not.

Character 1: Joe

- Joe is trying to help Mr Borthwick. He feels sorry for him because his shop does not have many customers.
- Joe also makes himself useful, by carrying the tin of spice.

Do you like Joe?

Explain to your class or group why you **do** or **do not** like Joe.

For practice (2)

Now think about the characters of Mr Borthwick and Mr Cassaroli.

Character 2: Mr Borthwick

- ★ Mr Borthwick says 'Excuse me' politely to Mr Cassaroli, after Mr Cassaroli shouts at him and tells him to go.
- ★ He does not give up, even when Mr Cassaroli walks away.

Write one or two sentences saying what you think about Mr Borthwick. Set it out like this:

I like / don't like* Mr Borthwick because ____________

* Score out the word you don't want to choose.

Character 3: Mr Cassaroli

- ★ Mr Cassaroli speaks angrily, 'How dare you enter my kitchen!'
- ★ He thinks he is very important and very clever. 'I am the great Cassaroli!' But he does not know the answer when they ask what the spice is.

Write one or two sentences saying what you think about Mr Cassaroli. Set it out like this:

I like / don't like* Mr Cassaroli because ____________

*Score out the word you don't want to choose.

Can you think . . .?

Can you think of a reason why the writer has named a character who is a chef 'Mr Cassaroli?' Imagine you are a writer. Can you think up some funny names for characters?

Pronouns

Pronouns take the place of nouns so you don't need to keep repeating them.

For example, in line 2 of the story, it said 'they' instead of 'Mr Borthwick and Joe'.

The words in this box are all pronouns:

he she it him her they them we us
I me you

Because they are nearly all about people, they are called **personal pronouns**.

For practice (3)

Write out the sentences, putting a pronoun into each of the spaces.

1 Joe and Mr Borthwick left the car and together ________ walked to the hotel.

2 A porter asked ____________ what ____________ wanted.

3 "Why are ____________ in my kitchen?" shouted Mr Cassaroli.

4 "____________ are looking for Mr Cassaroli," said Mr Borthwick.

5 "________ am the great Cassaroli," said the chef.

Part Two

Reading (Information)

Chapter 9

The Story of Walt Disney

Reading extract

Walt Disney was born in Chicago in 1901. When he was five years old his father moved the family to a farm. Walt and his sister Ruth were happy there. Later his father took ill and the family moved to Kansas City. Walt used to get up very early to deliver newspapers.

In 1923 Walt and his brother Roy set up a film studio in Hollywood. All they had was a small workshop and an old camera. They decided to make cartoon films. Walt did the drawings and his brother worked the camera.

At first things were difficult and the brothers had little money. Then Walt had an idea. While he was on a train from California to New York he was sketching in his drawing book. He came up with a character he called Mickey Mouse.

Mickey Mouse was the world's first cartoon character to appear in a film with sound. The film was a huge success and it made the Disney Studios large sums of →

Reading extract continued

money. Later Walt invented many other characters like Pluto, Donald Duck and Goofy.

In 1955 Disneyland opened in California. It was so popular that it had 30 million visitors in its first ten years. Then Walt started to build two new parks in Florida, Walt Disney World and Epcot. Sadly, he did not live to see these as he died in 1966.

The Disney Company has come up with many other ideas. It now owns other film companies and is the world's biggest publisher of books for children. In 1991 Disney made the world's first fully computer-animated film, 'Toy Story'. The company also owns a number of

Reading extract continued

television channels. There are 700 Disney stores across the world.

The Disney Company has come a long way since Walt did his first drawings of Mickey Mouse. In 2001 Disney World celebrated 100 years since Walt Disney's birth. There were special parades at the Disney parks.

Questions

Section A

Write down each sentence and choose the best ending from the box. The first one has been done for you, shown by a star *.

1 The cartoon character that first made Disney famous was

Donald Duck.
Mickey Mouse.*
Goofy.

2 Walt Disney was born in

1923.
1901.
1955.

3 Walt Disney set up a film studio with his

- father.
- sister.
- brother.

4 The studio was in

- Hollywood.
- Chicago.
- Kansas City.

5 Walt Disney came up with the idea for Mickey Mouse

- in his studio.
- on a train.
- on a farm.

6 The first Disney theme park was in

- Florida.
- California.
- New York.

Section B

Choose one word from the box to fit each space below. You will not need all the words. The first one is done for you, shown by a star *.

Your teacher will tell you if you need to write out the sentences or just the missing words.

cartoons	difficult	live	easy	camera
successful	visitors	ten	New York	studio
farm*	hundred	characters	newspapers	Florida

1 Walt Disney spent part of his childhood on a farm. *

2 Later he delivered __________ in Kansas City.

3 He opened a __________ with his brother Roy.

4 Walt Disney drew ____________ and Roy worked the _________.

5 At first things were ________ but the company became very ___________ after Walt came up with the idea of Mickey Mouse.

6 In the first ___ years 30 million _______ came to Disneyland.

7 Sadly, Walt Disney did not _______ to see the opening of the next two theme parks in ____________.

Section C

Use words from the passage or your own words to answer these questions.

1 The Disney family moved away from their farm because __________________.

2 Today the Disney company is the world's largest publisher of _______________.

3 Write down any **two** of the other things the Disney Company does (apart from making cartoon films).

4 What did Disneyland celebrate in 2001?

Taking a closer look

Verbs

'Doing words'

The words which tell us what people ***do*** are called 'verbs'.

Every sentence has a verb in it.

The story of Walt Disney tells us of many things Walt ***did***.

For example, when he was five he and his family ***moved*** to a farm.

The word '***moved***' tells us what the family ***did***.

For practice (1)

Find the verb in each of these sentences.

Hint

Ask what the person did.

1. Young Walt delivered newspapers.
2. Walt and his brother made cartoon films.
3. Walt drew the cartoons.
4. Walt's brother worked the camera.
5. Walt travelled by train to New York.

6 Walt sketched the Mickey Mouse cartoon.

7 Later, Walt invented many more cartoon animals.

8 In 1955, Disneyland opened in California.

9 Many people now visit Disneyland.

10 Walt built two parks in Florida.

For practice (2)

Fill each blank space with a verb (doing word) which makes sense.

1 Peter __________ in the sea on holiday.

2 Jenny __________ the ball to Tom.

3 Harry __________ his new pencil.

4 My dog __________ at strangers.

5 My Mum __________ a cake for my birthday.

Proper Nouns

Names given to people or places are called **proper nouns**. A proper noun begins with a capital letter.

Many proper nouns are used in the story about Walt Disney.

For practice (3)

From the passage, find:

five proper nouns for **places**

five proper nouns for **people**

You could use the names of characters from the Disney films.

You could draw boxes like these to write the names in.

For practice

Now make three more lists of your own:

- ★ **five** proper nouns for **places** (apart from the ones in the passage)
- ★ **five** proper nouns for **people** (apart from the ones in the passage)
- ★ **five** other proper nouns (you could use names of shops, cars, football teams, for example).

Chapter 10

Cats

Reading extract

The Cat Family

The cat family includes about 39 kinds of cat, from the tiger to the domestic cat. Depending on whether they live in the desert, grassland, forest, jungle – or in our homes – the different types of cat vary widely in size, colour, markings and way of life.

One of the smallest members of the cat family, the domestic cat is found nearly everywhere. These cats still sometimes mate with their ancestors, the wild cats. The tiger is the largest and most powerful of all the cats. Tigers cannot run quickly for long but are strong enough to tackle large prey. They are also fine swimmers.

Cat Behaviour

Cats communicate by purring, miaowing, or hissing. They also express themselves with their faces and with their body language. Domestic cats share much of their behaviour with their wild cousins. Yet they have had to →

Reading extract continued

adapt to share their territories with other animals and people.

Grooming

Both wild and domestic cats are extremely clean creatures. Regular grooming keeps a cat's coat glossy and healthy by getting rid of dirt, loose hair, and dead skin. Grooming also allows a cat to spread its scent all around its body. Usually grooming is the sign of a relaxed cat, but sometimes it shows a cat is nervous.

Choosing a cat

A cat may live for more than 15 years, and it needs a caring home for life. Once you have decided you can do →

Reading extract continued

this, you must choose the right companion. You may want to adopt an older cat, as kittens demand a lot of attention. However, kittens adapt easily to a new home.

Questions

Section A

The Cat Family

Write down the best ending for each sentence. The first one has been done for you, shown by a star *.

1 The number of kinds of cat is

more than one hundred.
less than ten.
about 39. *

2 The domestic cat is one of the [largest / smallest / strongest] of all the cats.

largest
smallest
strongest

3 Domestic cats sometimes mate with

tigers.
wild cats.
other animals.

4 The largest cat in the cat family is

the tiger.
the domestic cat.
the wild cat.

5 Tigers are good at

swimming.
running.
jumping.

Section B

Cat Behaviour

Choose a word from the box to fit each space. You will not need all the words. One is done for you, shown by a star *.

Your teacher will tell you if you should write out the sentences or just the missing words.

faces body communicate* adapt express territories share

1 Purring, miaowing and hissing are ways in which cats communicate.*

2 Cats also express themselves with ____________ language.

3 Domestic cats ____________ much of their behaviour with wild cats.

4 Cats have to share their ____________ with humans and other animals.

5 Cats have had to ____________ their behaviour to fit in with other animals and people.

Section C

Grooming

Find words from the passage to complete these sentences.

1 All cats are extremely ____________ creatures.

2 Regular grooming keeps a cat's coat ________ and ____________.

3 Grooming gets rid of ____________, ____________ and ____________.

4 Grooming also spreads ____________ over the cat's body.

5 Grooming is usually a sign that a cat is ____________, but it can also show it is ____________.

Section D

Choosing a cat

Write down the words which are needed to complete the story. You may use words from the passage or your own words.

Cats can live as long as ____1____ years, and so you must give your cat a ____2____ home for life. You must decide what kind of cat will be the right ____3____ for you. An ____4____ cat will not need as much attention as a kitten. However, a kitten will ____5____ more easily into a new home.

Taking a closer look

Adverbs

Adverb are words that tell us how something is done.

Many adverbs end in **–LY**.

In the story of 'Cats', it says tigers cannot run ***quickly***.

'***Quickly***' tells us more about how they run.

For practice (1)

Find an adverb from the first paragraph of Part 1 to fill this space:

★ Types of cat vary __________ in size.

Find an adverb from the last paragraph of Part 2 to fill this space:

★ Kittens adapt __________ to a new home.

For practice (2)

The words in the box are all adverbs.

greedily	sweetly	loudly	slowly	happily	fiercely
carefully	brightly				

Choose the best adverb from the box to fit each space.

1 When I got up the sun was shining __________.

2 Dan held the egg __________ in case it broke.

3 The children played __________ in the sandpit.

4 The birds sang __________ in the trees.

5 The fat man ate his dinner __________.

6 Sam shouted __________ for help when he fell.

7 The tired horse walked __________ up the steep hill.

8 The lion growled __________ at the hunter.

Chapter 11

Football

Reading extract

Football is the most popular sport in the world. It is played in more than 200 countries. Top clubs can attract huge numbers of fans to watch them play. The Spanish club Barcelona's ground has seats for as many as 115,000 fans.

One reason why football is so popular is that in some ways it is a simple game. Anyone can play and it can be played on almost any surface. Even the world's poorest

Reading extract continued

children can have fun kicking a ball in the street, on grass or on the beach.

The rules of football are also simple. Each team has 11 players. The game lasts for 90 minutes. The aim is to get the ball past the other side's goalkeeper and into the goal. The rules of the game may be easy to understand, but plenty of skill is needed to play well.

The history of football goes back a long time. It was not until 1863 that the rules of football were agreed on. In that year the English Football Association was set up and football and rugby became different sports.

The most important football competition today is the World Cup. It was first held in 1930. Thanks to television, everyone in the world can enjoy the matches. In 2002 more than one sixth of the world's population watched the World Cup finals.

But football today is not only about sport. It is also to do with making money. Football clubs can become rich by allowing matches to be shown on television. Money can also be made from selling items like football strips. This allows the clubs to pay large sums of money to their players. Some people think these players are paid too much. They say that it is unfair that footballers are paid far more money than other people who do more important kinds of work.

Questions

Section A

Write down each sentence and choose the best ending from the box. The first answer has been done for you, shown by a star *.

1 The aim of a football game is to get the ball past the other side's

players.
goalkeeper.*
fans.

2 A football game lasts for

200
11
90

minutes.

3 Barcelona is a football team from

Spain.
England.
Italy.

4 Top football clubs can attract huge numbers of

players.
goalkeepers.
fans.

5 The World Cup was first held in

1863.
1930.
2002.

Section B

Choose **one word** from the box to fill each space below.

You will not need all the words. One is done for you, shown by a star *.

Your teacher will tell you if you need to write out the whole paragraph or just the missing words.

unfair beach children grass difficult important Association easy skill street played* popular money fair

Football can be played* on any surface. One reason why football is so ____1____ is that it can be played by anyone. Even the world's poorest ____2____ can have fun kicking a ball in the ____3____, on ____4____ or on the ____5____. The rules of football are ____6____ to understand. These rules were agreed by the English Football ____7____ in 1863. Plenty of ____8____ is needed to become a good footballer.

Today footballers are paid large amounts of ____9____.

Many people think this is ____10____ as other people who do ____11____ work are not paid as much.

Section C

Find words or phrases from the passage to answer these questions.

1 The most important football competition today is called ______________.

2 Everyone can enjoy watching the matches in this competition on ________.

3 Huge numbers of people around the world watched the ________________ of this football competition in 2002.

4 Two ways that football clubs can become rich are:

a) ______________________________

b) ______________________________

Taking a closer look

Nouns

Singular and plural

When a noun means one thing it is ***singular***.

When a noun means more than one thing it is ***plural***.

Most times, you add **–s** to a noun to make it plural.

For example,

Car is singular – meaning one car

Cars is plural – meaning more than one car

For practice (1)

Write down the plurals of these words. You will find all the words in the story.

1 country ___________	**6** rule ___________
2 club ___________	**7** player ___________
3 fan ___________	**8** sport ___________
4 seat ___________	**9** match ___________
5 child ___________	**10** footballer ___________

For practice (2)

Write down the singular of these plurals:

1 Two bags, one ___________

2 Two flies, one ___________

3 Two fishes, one ___________

4 Two sheep, one ___________

5 Two men, one ___________

6 Two geese, one ___________

7 Two mice, one ___________

8 Two wolves, one ___________

Chapter 12

The Roman World

Reading extract

The Romans were one of the great peoples of the ancient world. The city of Rome was the capital of an empire that stretched across Europe, Asia Minor and North Africa. The earliest Romans were an Iron Age tribe in central Italy. They built a fortress around seven hills near the River Tiber.

The Romans were clever at war. They had a powerful army led by skilful generals. They also became good sailors and built a fleet of warships. They defeated people who lived nearby, then offered them peace and the chance to become Roman citizens. By the year 30 BC, the Romans controlled all the lands around the Mediterranean Sea.

The peoples of the Roman Empire were united by a shared way of life. The language of the Empire was the Roman tongue of Latin. The coins in use had the head of the Emperor on them. One set of laws was used all over the Empire. All the lands in the Empire were defended by the Roman army.

→

Reading extract continued

The Romans liked to live in towns. In every Roman city, they built temples to their gods. There was a large open market place called the forum where their merchants could meet. Most Roman towns had public baths where people could go to wash and meet their friends. All the towns and cities of the Empire were linked together by roads that were straight and well-made. These roads carried the army, goods and important messages across the Empire.

Questions

Section A

Write down each sentence and choose the best ending from the box. The first one has been done for you, shown by a star *.

1 The city of Rome is in

- Asia Minor.
- Italy.*
- North Africa.

2 The Romans were one of the great peoples of

- Asia.
- the ancient world.
- modern times.

3 The city of Rome was surrounded by

- seven hills.
- other cities.
- the sea.

4 The leaders of the Roman army were called

- generals.
- sailors.
- citizens.

5 In their cities the Romans built temples for their

- friends.
- merchants.
- gods.

Section B

Choose **one** word from the box to fit each space below. You will not need all the words. The first one is done for you, shown by a star *.

Your teacher will tell you if you need to write out the sentences or just the missing words.

soldiers	*towns*	*citizens*	*laws*	*forum*	*baths*
villages	*united*	*peoples**	*warships*		

1 The Romans were one of the great peoples* of the ancient world.

2 The Roman armies defeated their enemies and offered them the chance to become Roman __________.

3 The people of the Roman Empire were ________ because they shared the same way of life.

4 One set of _________ was used throughout the Roman Empire.

5 The lands of the Empire were defended by Roman ________.

6 The Romans liked to live in _________.

7 The main market place in a Roman city was called the ________.

Section C

Use words from the passage to answer these questions.

1 The city of Rome was built around the River ______.

2 By the year 30 BC the Romans were in control of all the lands around the ________________ Sea.

3 The language used in the Roman Empire was ________.

4 On Roman coins there was a picture of the head of the ___________.

5 The roads that linked the cities of the Empire together were _________ and ___________.

6 Romans used to go to public baths to ________ and to meet their _________.

7 Roman roads carried ____________, goods and ____________ across the Empire.

Taking a closer look

Collective Nouns

Some nouns are the names of ***groups*** of things.

They are called ***collective*** nouns.

For example, in the story, there was 'a ***fleet*** of warships'.

'***fleet***' is a collective noun – it is a group of ships.

★ Can you find a word in the **second** paragraph of the story which means a group of soldiers?

For practice (1)

Think of words to fill in the spaces. The words you use should all be **collective** nouns.

1 I gave my Mum a __________ of flowers.

2 There was a __________ of sheep in the field.

3 My dog had a __________ of puppies.

4 We played 'Snap' with a __________ of cards.

5 My Dad has bought a __________ of golf clubs.

Adjectives

The word 'Roman' is an adjective formed from the proper noun, Rome.

Adjectives formed from proper nouns also begin with a **capital letter**.

For practice (2)

Write down the proper nouns these adjectives come from.

	Noun	Adjective
1	___________	English
2	___________	Italian
3	___________	Scottish
4	___________	German
6	___________	Swedish

For practice (3)

Can you form an adjective from each of these proper nouns?

	Noun	Adjective
1	Poland	___________
2	Greece	___________
3	Ireland	___________
4	Norway	___________
5	Wales	___________

An exception!

Do you know the adjective that describes things from Holland? The word is quite different.

Holland ___________

Chapter 13

Making Do in World War Two

Reading extract

When war broke out, Britain was short of many important war supplies such as petrol, food and metal for weapons. In 1940, German submarines sank hundreds of supply ships carrying food from abroad, many of them off the west coast of Scotland at the mouth of the River Clyde.

The government was worried that Britain might be starved into surrender. Food had to be rationed to make sure everyone got a fair share. Every family was given a Ration Book. It was made up of paper tokens. People had to register with their local butcher and grocer. They had to have the right number of tokens to buy rationed foods that were in short supply. These included sugar, butter and meat. Luxury foods such as sweets and fresh fruit were almost impossible to find. Scottish children grew up during the war years never knowing what an orange or banana looked or tasted like.

There was no shortage of the foods than could be grown in Scotland, such as potatoes, turnips and barley. Even →

Reading extract continued

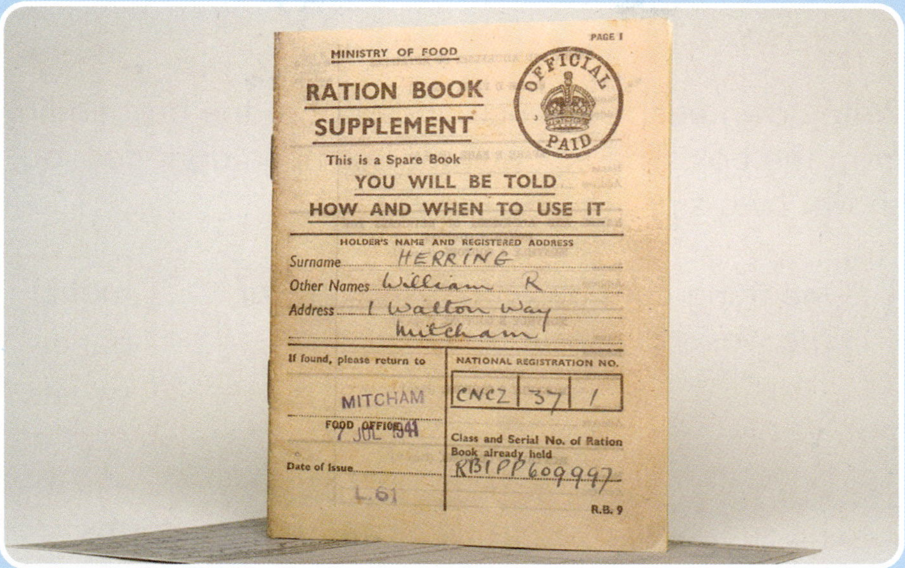

in towns, people were encouraged to 'dig for victory' by planting vegetables in their gardens. Councils sometimes ploughed up local parks to plant 'greens'. Fish was never rationed, so many Scottish communities around the coast had a plentiful supply of food from fishing. Even so, nothing could be wasted. All food scraps were kept to be made into a 'hot pot' or fed to the pigs.

Some Scots tried to vary their diet by using unusual foods such as nettle soup or dandelion fritters. Many Scottish children grew up on 'potted heid', meat boiled off the head of a sheep or cows and then set in jelly. Whale meat was tried at one point during the war but it was not popular. Many people kept rabbits and pigeons as a way of getting extra meat.

Questions

Section A

Write down each sentence and choose the best ending from the box. The first answer has been done for you, shown by a star *.

1 One thing considered a luxury in war time was

> meat.
> barley.
> sweets.*

2 The supply ships were destroyed by

> storms.
> submarines.
> planes.

3 During the war people were unable to buy

> butter.
> meat.
> fresh fruits.

4 Some of the foods that were not in short supply included

> bananas.
> potatoes.
> oranges.

5 To help with the food shortage, people who lived in towns were encouraged to 'dig for victory' by

> planting their own vegetables.
> going fishing.
> eating dandelions and nettles.

Section B

Choose one word from the box to fit each space below. You will not need all the words. One is done for you, shown by a star *.

Ration	luxury	surrender	Clyde*	share
government	vegetables	register	unusual	

1 Many supply ships were sunk near the mouth of the River Clyde.*

2 The ____________ thought that the enemy wanted to starve Britain into ___________.

3 To make sure everyone received a fair _________, every family was given a _________ book.

4 To get their supply of meat, people had to __________ with their local butcher.

5 Some parks were ploughed up so that more __________ could be grown.

Section C

Find words from the passage to answer these questions.

1 During the second world war metal had to be brought to Britain from other countries to make __________ .

2 A ration book contained paper ______________.

3 During the war luxury foods were __________ to find.

4 People who lived near the Scottish coast had a plentiful supply of ______ to eat.

5 As food was in short supply it was important that nothing was ______________.

6 ________ meat was tried at one point during the war but it was not ______________.

7 As a way of getting extra meat, many people kept __________ and ______________.

Section D

Find words to fill in the gaps, using **one** word in each space. You may use your own words or words from the passage.

Your teacher will tell you if you need to write out the whole paragraph or just the missing words.

Because food was so hard to get, many Scots tried to add variety to their _____1_____ by trying _____2_____ foods made out of ingredients like nettles or dandelions. Children were given 'potted heid', meat that was _____3_____ from the head of a cow or sheep and then set in _____4_____. Leftover food was kept and fed to _____5_____ .

Taking a closer look

Words and their Meanings (1)

General and particular

Try this example:

★ Gun, sword and spear are all __________.

Can you think of a word to fill the space?

Hint

The word you need is in the first paragraph of the story, Making Do in World War Two.

The word is 'weapons'. It is a **general** word, while gun, sword and spear are all **particular** things.

For practice (1)

Write down the ***general*** word for these ***particular*** things.

Hint

The words you need are all in the story.

1 submarine, steamer and ferry are all __________

2 oranges, apples and bananas are all __________

3 lamb, beef and chicken are all __________

4 cod, haddock and sole are all __________

5 cabbage, peas and beans are all __________

For practice (2)

Write down **three** particular examples for these general words.

1 __________ , __________ and __________ are all foods.

2 __________ , __________ and __________ are all flowers.

3 __________ , __________ and __________ are all metals.

4 __________ , __________ and __________ are all animals

5 __________ , __________ and __________ are all crops.

Chapter 14

What Are Dinosaurs?

Reading extract

Part 1

About 225 million years ago, a new group of reptiles appeared on Earth. Like all reptiles, they had waterproof, scaly skin and young that hatched from eggs. These were the dinosaurs. For the next 160 million years they ruled the Earth before finally becoming extinct.

Dinosaurs came in many shapes and sizes. A group of dinosaurs called the sauropods were the largest land animals that ever lived. The Barosaurus was heavier than eight elephants and more than 24 metres long. The smallest dinosaurs were chicken-sized. Large or small, all would have been wary of hungry meat eaters. Some dinosaurs had armoured skin for protection. Others were fast runners and could escape predators by fleeing to safer ground. There were many more herbivores (plant eaters) than carnivores (meat eaters) in the dinosaur world. A herbivore called Stegosaurus had a sharp beak for cropping leaves off plants.

Reading extract continued

Part 2

Everything we know about dinosaurs is based on their fossilised remains. These are pieced together to make the skeletons we see in museums. Fossils are the remains of ancient living things preserved in rocks.

As scientists understand better how dinosaurs lived, museums try to arrange dinosaur skeletons in a variety of poses. Scientists at the American Museum of Natural History in New York built an exciting display. They showed a Barosaurus skeleton rearing up, defending its young against an attacking Allosaurus. As the fossil

Reading extract continued

bones of Barosaurus were very fragile and too heavy to display in such a pose, a lightweight replica of the skeleton was made.

Dinosaurs laid eggs, like most other reptiles as well as birds. In recent years, scientists have discovered dinosaur nesting sites which helped them know more about the early life of dinosaurs. These sites showed that some young stayed in their nests, cared for by adults, until they were old enough to leave. They also showed that dinosaurs, like many birds, used the same nesting sites year after year.

Questions

Section A

Write down the best ending for each sentence.

A Like all reptiles, the dinosaurs

- lived in water.
- were meat-eaters.
- hatched young from eggs.

B All dinosaurs were afraid of

- elephants.
- meat-eaters.
- herbivores.

C Scientists learned about dinosaurs from

- fossils.
- museums.
- displays.

D The real skeleton of the barosaurus could not be used in a display because

- it was too big.
- it was rearing up.
- it was too fragile.

E Dinosaurs were like birds because

- they made nests.
- they could fly.
- they had feathers.

Section B

Here is a summary of Part 1 of the passage. Write down the words which are needed to complete it. You may use words from the passage or your own words.

Dinosaurs lived 225 _____1_____ years ago. They ruled the earth until they became _____2_____. Dinosaurs came in many different _____3_____. The smallest dinosaur was no bigger than a _____4_____ . Most of the dinosaurs ate _____5_____.

Section C

Find a phrase on the right to match each word in the list.

Write down the word, then beside it write the letter with the correct meaning.

Some phrases will be left over.

1 sauropods______	A was heavier than eight elephants
2 herbivores______	B were the largest land animals that ever lived
3 stegosaurus _____	C attacked other dinosaurs
4 fossils ______	D had armoured skin for protection
5 allosaurus______	E had a sharp beak for cropping leaves
	F are the remains of ancient things preserved in rocks
	G are plant eaters

Section D

Find words from Part 2 of the passage which will complete these sentences.

Your teacher will tell you if you need to write out the whole sentences or just the missing words.

1 All we know about dinosaurs comes from their __________ remains.

2 Museums set up dinosaur skeletons in a variety of __________.

3 The Barosaurus looked as if it was __________ its young from the Allosaurus.

4 Because the real bones of the Barosaurus were so heavy and fragile, the museum made a lightweight __________ of its skeleton.

5 The study of dinosaur __________ helped scientists know more about the early life of dinosaurs.

Taking a closer look

Words and their Meanings (2)

Words with like meanings

Some words mean almost the same as others.

For example, in the story, instead of saying 'dinosaurs ***appeared*** on earth', you could say, 'dinosaurs ***arrived*** on earth.'

'***appeared***' and '***arrived***' mean almost the same.

For practice (1)

Can you match up the words which have the same meanings?

The words in the list below were all in the story. Write them down. Then pick a word from the box which you think means the same and write it opposite. You will need to use all the words in the box.

1 wary ____________

2 fragile ____________

3 replica ____________

4 discovered ____________

5 exciting ____________

6 defending ____________

7 sites ____________

8 stayed ____________

9 poses ____________

10 based ____________

positions	found	founded	nervous	copy
protecting	brittle	thrilling	places	remained

For practice (2)

How many words can you think of with the same meaning as these?

Draw four boxes like this. Then write the words in the boxes.

You could try this with a partner or a group.

large	**small**
happy	**sad**

Chapter 15

Festivals

Reading extract

1 Flags are flying, bands play loud music, fireworks explode in the sky. There are feasts and street parties. People put on their best clothes or wear special costumes, fancy dress or masks. All over the world, people gather together to celebrate festivals, fairs, carnivals and holidays.

2 Some festivals are just for fun. Others are more serious. They may mark the passing of a season, or be part of our religious beliefs. Some festivals are to remember great events of the past, or the lives of famous people. All over the world, special events are held for birthdays, growing up, getting married and dying. These may be small family gatherings or times when large groups of friends or even whole villages come together.

3 Presents are often given for birthdays. In China, an egg that is dyed red is given to a one-month-old baby as a symbol of happiness. In parts of Africa, teenage girls and boys must paint their bodies to show that they are ready to become grown-ups. For weddings,

Reading extract continued

people everywhere wear their best clothes, give gifts and hold feasts. Funerals are sad, but in some countries they are happy events, too. People celebrate the life that has come to an end or gather to wish the dead person well in the spirit world.

4 Midsummer, autumn and the dark days of winter have their own celebrations. Many of these date back thousands of years and include dancing, music, bonfires and processions. Festivals around the world mark the sowing of seed, the coming of the rains and the harvest. Today, in countries from eastern Asia to Western Europe, fishermen ask priests to bless their boats and nets each season.

Reading extract continued

5 We don't always need a special reason to enjoy ourselves. Many festivals have no other purpose than making merry. Sometimes, the reason for holding them has been long forgotten. Halloween is a scary fun festival, held on 31st October. It dates back to an ancient Celtic festival, when people thought that the spirits of the dead could be seen. The Celts were originally head hunters who hung the heads of their enemies in their huts. At Halloween we still decorate our houses with heads made of pumpkins or turnips.

Questions

Section A

Write down the best ending to each of these sentences.

1 Festivals are held
- in Asia and Western Europe.
- mainly in China.
- all over the world.

2 Festivals
- are serious events.
- can be both fun and serious.
- are now just for fun.

3 In China, an egg dyed red is given to

- a baby on its birthday.
- a one month old baby.
- a teenager growing up.

4 Festivals which mark the seasons of the year

- are mainly held in spring.
- are no longer held anywhere.
- are thousands of years old.

5 The festival of Halloween began

- as an ancient festival of head-hunters.
- as a modern festival of pumpkins and turnips.
- in recent times as a fun festival.

Section B

The answers to the following questions can be found in the **first paragraph**.

Use words or phrases from the text in your answers.

1 Write down **two** sounds you might hear at festivals.

2 Write down **two** things people wear at festivals.

3 Find **three** other words in the first paragraph which are similar in meaning to 'festival'.

Section C

The answers to the next questions can be found in paragraphs 2, 3 and 4. Write out the correct answers.

1 Which **two** of these reasons are mentioned in the passage for holding a festival?
a birthday; starting school; building a house; getting married; leaving home.

2 Find the **one** thing teenage children in Africa do to show they are ready to become adults:
wear their best clothes; paint their bodies; hold a feast.

3 Which **one** of these seasons of the year is not mentioned as having its own festival:
spring; summer; autumn; winter.

Section D

The answers to the next questions are to be found in the **last** paragraph.

1 On what date is the festival of Halloween celebrated?

2 Write down **two** words the writer uses to describe the festival of Halloween.

3 Where did the Celts hang the heads of their enemies?

4 What **two** things are used today to decorate houses at Halloween?

Section E

Here is a summary of the passage. Some of the words have been missed out. Write down the words which are needed to complete the story. You may use your own words or words from the passage.

Your teacher will tell you if you need to write out the whole summary or just the missing words.

Festivals range in size from small _____ 1 _____ gatherings to events which whole _____ 2 _____ may attend.

Birthdays and weddings are often marked by giving _____ 3 _____. Funerals can be sad, but they may also be _____ 4 _____ events if they are held to _____ 5 _____ the life that has ended.

Farmers may celebrate events such as the _____ 6 _____ of seed. Fishermen in many countries ask _____ 7 _____ to bless their boats and nets.

Some festivals are now just held for fun as the reasons for holding them have been _____ 8 _____. However, Halloween began as an ancient festival of the Celts who hung the _____ 9 _____ of their enemies in their huts. Now we decorate our houses with _____ 10 _____.

Taking a closer look

Commas

Commas show ***pauses*** in a sentence. They make sentences easier to read and understand.

Commas are used to separate things in a list.

For example:

festivals, fairs, carnivals and holidays

You should not put a comma before 'and'.

For practice (1)

Write out these sentences, putting in commas.

Hint

All of these lists are in the story and you can check if you have put the commas in the right places.

1 Events are held for birthdays growing up getting married and dying.

2 People wear their best clothes give gifts and hold feasts.

3 Midsummer autumn and winter have their own celebrations.

4 The festivals include dancing music bonfires and processions.

5 Festivals mark the sowing of seed the coming of the rains and the harvest.

Spelling

Words ending in –y

To change singular to plural, remember this rule:

★ Change the 'y' to 'i' and add 'es'.

For example,

party – parties

For practice (2)

Use this rule to form plurals.

	Singular	Plural
1	sky	____________
2	family	____________
3	baby	____________
4	country	____________
5	enemy	____________

Exception!

If the letter before the 'y' is a vowel, like 'a', 'e' or 'o', just add –s.

For example,

holiday – holidays.

For practice (3)

Remember the rule for exceptions and form plurals from these words.

	Singular	Plural
1	tray	______________
2	birthday	______________
3	toy	______________
4	ray	______________
5	boy	______________

Chapter 16

Dragons

Reading extract

1 Stories about dragons occur everywhere in the world. All lands have legends of these powerful creatures. Most stories about dragons mention their fire-breathing abilities. They probably arose from people's memories of thunder and lightning or erupting volcanoes. But while the dragons of the west are usually described as cruel, evil creatures, those of the east are often said to be kind and gentle. Several ancient religions had dragons at the centre of their

Reading extract continued

beliefs. People believed that dragons created the earth and human beings as well as controlling the wind, rain, rivers and seas.

2 Dragon-slaying legends occur in lands where the monsters were said to be evil and cruel. In these tales, good overcomes evil. Of all the dragon-slayers, St George, the patron saint of England, is best known. St George, a knight in shining armour, was born near Jerusalem. Travelling around Europe and the Middle East on his horse, he slew many dragons and rescued young women.

3 Of all the dragons in the world, the Chinese ones were the most respected. Unlike many western dragons, those of the Far East were harmless, good, kind, intelligent and friendly. The Chinese believed in many different types of dragon, and almost every part of daily life has its own special guardian dragon. The years in the Chinese calendar are named after different animals and one of these is the dragon.

4 Dragons have been brought to life in many forms. Dragons were woven or embroidered on Chinese emperors' robes and carved on Vikings' long-ships. All over the world they appear on buildings, but they are

Reading extract continued

especially common in the Far East. Here, buildings are decorated with dragon roof ornaments, tiles and steps. Bridges bear dragon shapes in honour of the river dragons. In Europe, dragons are used in old Christian churches to ward off evil spirits and to represent the devil and evil. They are also used to decorate furniture, china and other ornaments.

Questions

Section A

Underline the best ending to each sentence.

1 Stories about dragons are told

- in China.
- in England.
- in the Middle East.
- everywhere in the world.

2 Legends about St George said that

- he killed many dragons.
- he killed only one dragon.
- he rescued children.
- he travelled in China.

3 St George was born

- in England.
- in the Middle East.
- in China.
- in Jerusalem.

4 Chinese dragons

- are very like western dragons.
- are harmless and friendly.
- are mostly evil and cruel.
- are all the same type.

5 Dragons were used in old Christian churches

- to decorate the roof.
- to decorate furniture.
- to keep away evil spirits.
- as ornaments.

Section B

The answers to the next questions are all in the first paragraph.

Use a word or phrase from the first paragraph to fill each of the spaces.

Your teacher will tell you if you need to write out the sentences or just the missing words.

1 People thought dragons breathed fire because of their memories of

____

and ______________________________________.

2 **Two** adjectives the writer uses to describe the dragons of the west are ____________ and ____________.

3 **Two** adjectives the writer uses to describe the dragons of the east are ____________ and ____________.

4 Some religious people believed dragons had created____________ and ____________.

5 Write down **four** things some people believed were controlled by dragons.

1 ____________ 2 ____________

3 ____________ 4 ____________.

Section C

The next questions are about St George and the answers can all be found in paragraph 2.

1 St George is the **patron** saint of which country?

2 What does the writer say that St George **wears**?

3 Write down **two places** where St George travelled.

Section D

The answers to the next questions can be found in paragraphs 3 and 4.

Find a word or phrase from the passage for each space.

1 In China, almost all parts of daily life had a special ____________ dragon.

2 One of the years in the Chinese ____________ is called the year of the dragon.

3 Dragons were used to decorate the robes of the Chinese ____________.

4 Dragons were carved on the ships of the ____________.

5 Bridges have dragon shapes to honour the ____________dragons.

Section E

Here is a summary of the passage. Some of the words have been missed out. Write down **one or more words** to fill each space. You may use your own words or words from the passage.

Legends about dragons are told all over the ____1____. Most stories mention that dragons can ____2____ fire. Some ancient religions believed that dragons had ____3____ the world and its people, and they thought they ____4____ the weather.

In western countries, people ____5____ dragons were evil and cruel creatures, and there were many ____6____ about knights like St George slaying these monsters. On his travels, it was said that St George also rescued ____7____.

However, the ____8____ believed that dragons were harmless, good, kind and intelligent. In the Far East, many buildings and bridges are ____9____ with ornamental dragons. In Europe, dragons are sometimes to be found in old Christian ____10____. Dragons were also ____11____ to decorate furniture, china and similar objects.

Taking a closer look

Contrast

When things are very different, they are said to ***contrast***.

For example, ***good*** contrasts with ***evil***.

In the story, the dragons of the east contrasted with the dragons of the west.

Dragons of the east were ***kind and gentle***, while dragons of the west were ***cruel and evil***.

For practice (1)

Write down words which contrast with these. There may be more than one correct answer!

1. east
2. shining
3. white
4. friendly
5. fire
6. cold
7. round
8. ancient
9. intelligent
10. harmless

For practice (2)

Think of more pairs of words which contrast with each other.

Write them down in a list. You could do this with a partner or a group.

Spelling

Words saying 'ee'

Words with the sound 'ee' in them are sometimes spelt with the letters 'ie' or 'ei'.

This easy rhyme will help you to remember which way round they should go:

'I' before 'E' except after 'C'

For example, 'belief' has 'ie' but 'receive' has 'ei' since it comes after a 'c'.

For practice (3)

Complete these words, using 'ie' or 'ei:

1 ch___f	**5** rec___pt
2 dec___ve	**6** gr___f
3 th___f	**7** rel___f
4 bel___ve	**8** perc___ve